EMMANUEL JOSEPH

The Ethical Edge, Balancing Innovation, Psychology, and Cultural Awareness in Business

Copyright © 2025 by Emmanuel Joseph

All rights reserved. No part of this publication may be reproduced, stored or transmitted in any form or by any means, electronic, mechanical, photocopying, recording, scanning, or otherwise without written permission from the publisher. It is illegal to copy this book, post it to a website, or distribute it by any other means without permission.

First edition

This book was professionally typeset on Reedsy.
Find out more at reedsy.com

Contents

1. Chapter 1: The Evolution of Business Ethics — 1
2. Chapter 2: Innovation and Its Ethical Implications — 3
3. Chapter 3: Understanding Consumer Psychology — 5
4. Chapter 4: Cultural Awareness in Global Markets — 7
5. Chapter 5: Corporate Social Responsibility and Ethical... — 9
6. Chapter 6: The Role of Ethics in Marketing and Advertising — 11
7. Chapter 7: Ethical Decision-Making in the Digital Age — 13
8. Chapter 8: Building an Ethical Corporate Culture — 15
9. Chapter 9: Ethical Supply Chain Management — 17
10. Chapter 10: The Importance of Ethics in Corporate Governance — 19
11. Chapter 11: Ethical Considerations in Financial Management — 21
12. Chapter 12: Balancing Profit and Purpose — 23
13. Chapter 13: Ethics in Technology and Innovation — 25
14. Chapter 14: Navigating Ethical Challenges in the Global... — 27
15. Chapter 15: The Role of Ethics in Crisis Management — 29
16. Chapter 16: The Future of Business Ethics — 31
17. Chapter 17: Embracing Ethical Principles for a Better Future — 33

1

Chapter 1: The Evolution of Business Ethics

The journey of business ethics has evolved over centuries, beginning from the barter system to the contemporary digital economy. In ancient times, ethical business was tied to personal honor and reputation, with merchants adhering to trust-based principles. As industries emerged during the Industrial Revolution, the complexity of ethical considerations grew, encompassing labor rights, environmental impact, and corporate governance. Today, ethics in business transcends mere compliance with laws and regulations; it embodies a commitment to social responsibility, sustainability, and inclusivity, requiring businesses to balance profit motives with moral imperatives.

As economies grew and global trade expanded, ethical business practices began to integrate into legal frameworks and corporate policies. The 20th century saw the rise of corporate social responsibility (CSR), where companies started to acknowledge their broader societal impact. This era marked a shift from profit-centric models to stakeholder-inclusive approaches, considering the interests of employees, communities, and the environment. The advent of digital technology and globalization further amplified the importance of ethics in business, as companies now operate in diverse cultural landscapes and face heightened scrutiny from informed consumers and stakeholders.

The complexity of ethical dilemmas has increased with technological advancements, prompting businesses to adopt comprehensive ethical guidelines and frameworks. Issues such as data privacy, artificial intelligence ethics, and sustainable sourcing practices are now at the forefront of business discussions. Companies are expected to demonstrate transparency, accountability, and a commitment to ethical principles in every aspect of their operations. As society continues to evolve, so too must the ethical standards that guide businesses, ensuring they remain relevant and impactful in addressing contemporary challenges.

Today, ethical business practices are no longer optional; they are a necessity for long-term success and reputation management. Companies that prioritize ethics and integrity are better positioned to build trust with their stakeholders, foster customer loyalty, and attract top talent. As the business landscape continues to evolve, the role of ethics in shaping corporate strategies and decision-making processes will only grow in significance. By embracing ethical principles, businesses can navigate the complexities of the modern world with integrity and purpose.

2

Chapter 2: Innovation and Its Ethical Implications

Innovation drives progress, but its ethical implications cannot be overlooked. The introduction of groundbreaking technologies can lead to significant shifts in societal norms, employment, and resource allocation. For instance, artificial intelligence and automation have the potential to enhance productivity but also raise concerns about privacy, job displacement, and economic inequality. Ethical innovation requires a conscientious approach, ensuring that advancements align with broader societal values and address potential consequences. Businesses must engage stakeholders, anticipate risks, and implement safeguards to ensure that innovation fosters positive change.

The rapid pace of innovation often outstrips the development of regulatory frameworks, creating ethical gray areas that businesses must navigate. Issues such as the ethical use of data, intellectual property rights, and the environmental impact of new technologies require careful consideration. Companies must adopt proactive measures to address these challenges, including conducting ethical impact assessments, engaging with diverse stakeholders, and fostering a culture of responsibility and accountability. By integrating ethical considerations into the innovation process, businesses can ensure that their advancements contribute to the greater good.

Ethical innovation also involves balancing the pursuit of profit with the well-being of society and the environment. Companies must consider the long-term implications of their innovations, including potential unintended consequences and the broader social and environmental impact. This requires a commitment to sustainable practices, ethical sourcing, and responsible marketing. By prioritizing ethical principles, businesses can create value that extends beyond financial gains, contributing to the overall well-being of society and the planet.

Collaboration and transparency are key to fostering ethical innovation. Businesses must work closely with regulators, industry peers, and civil society organizations to develop and implement ethical guidelines and standards. Open dialogue and collaboration can help identify potential risks and create solutions that promote responsible innovation. By embracing a collaborative approach, companies can navigate the complexities of the modern business landscape with integrity and purpose, ensuring that their innovations contribute to a better future for all.

3

Chapter 3: Understanding Consumer Psychology

Consumer psychology plays a pivotal role in shaping business strategies. Understanding the motivations, preferences, and behaviors of consumers allows businesses to design products and marketing campaigns that resonate deeply. Ethical considerations emerge when businesses leverage psychological insights for persuasive techniques, such as targeted advertising and personalized experiences. Transparency and respect for consumer autonomy are essential, ensuring that marketing practices do not exploit vulnerabilities or manipulate choices. By adopting ethical principles in consumer psychology, businesses can build trust and foster long-term relationships with their customers.

In today's digital age, the availability of vast amounts of consumer data has transformed the way businesses approach marketing and product development. Advanced analytics and artificial intelligence enable companies to gain deeper insights into consumer behavior, allowing for highly targeted and personalized marketing strategies. However, the ethical use of consumer data is paramount. Companies must prioritize data privacy, obtain informed consent, and ensure transparency in how data is collected, used, and shared. By adhering to ethical data practices, businesses can build trust and maintain positive relationships with their customers.

The ethical application of consumer psychology also involves avoiding manipulative tactics and ensuring that marketing practices are fair and honest. Techniques such as deceptive advertising, hidden fees, and pressure tactics can erode consumer trust and damage a company's reputation. Instead, businesses should focus on creating value for consumers through honest communication, transparent pricing, and high-quality products and services. By prioritizing ethical marketing practices, companies can build lasting relationships with their customers and foster brand loyalty.

Consumer psychology also plays a crucial role in product development and innovation. By understanding consumer needs, preferences, and pain points, businesses can create products and services that genuinely address those needs and improve the consumer experience. Ethical considerations should guide every stage of the product development process, from concept to launch. This includes conducting thorough market research, engaging with diverse consumer groups, and incorporating feedback to ensure that products are safe, effective, and aligned with consumer values. By adopting an ethical approach to consumer psychology, businesses can create products that resonate with consumers and contribute to their overall well-being.

4

Chapter 4: Cultural Awareness in Global Markets

In the interconnected global economy, cultural awareness is paramount for ethical business conduct. Every culture encompasses unique values, beliefs, and practices that influence consumer behavior and business interactions. Misunderstandings or insensitivity to cultural differences can lead to reputational damage and ethical breaches. For example, marketing campaigns that overlook cultural nuances may inadvertently offend or alienate certain demographics. Ethical business practices require cultural competence, involving respectful engagement, adaptation, and collaboration with diverse communities. By prioritizing cultural awareness, businesses can navigate the complexities of global markets ethically and effectively.

Cultural awareness involves understanding and appreciating the diversity of cultural perspectives and practices. This requires a commitment to ongoing education, open-mindedness, and a willingness to learn from others. Businesses must invest in cultural training for their employees, foster inclusive work environments, and seek to understand the unique needs and preferences of their diverse customer base. By embracing cultural diversity, companies can create more inclusive and effective business strategies that resonate with a global audience.

Ethical business conduct in global markets also involves respecting local customs, traditions, and regulatory frameworks. Companies must be mindful of the cultural context in which they operate and ensure that their practices align with local values and expectations. This includes ethical sourcing, fair labor practices, and environmentally sustainable operations. By demonstrating cultural respect and ethical responsibility, businesses can build positive relationships with local communities and contribute to their social and economic development.

Collaboration and partnership are essential for navigating cultural complexities in global markets. Businesses should seek to engage with local stakeholders, including community leaders, NGOs, and government agencies, to gain insights and build trust. Collaborative efforts can help identify and address potential ethical challenges, create mutually beneficial solutions, and promote sustainable development. By fostering partnerships and cultural understanding, companies can navigate the global business landscape with integrity and contribute to a more inclusive and ethical world.

5

Chapter 5: Corporate Social Responsibility and Ethical Leadership

Corporate Social Responsibility (CSR) embodies the notion that businesses have an obligation to contribute positively to society. Ethical leadership is the cornerstone of effective CSR, driving initiatives that address social, environmental, and economic challenges. Ethical leaders prioritize the well-being of stakeholders, making decisions that align with the values of integrity, transparency, and accountability. They foster a culture of ethical behavior within their organizations, encouraging employees to act responsibly and uphold ethical standards. By integrating CSR into their business strategies, ethical leaders create value not only for shareholders but also for communities, the environment, and society at large.

Effective CSR requires a strategic approach, aligning philanthropic efforts with core business objectives. Companies must identify key areas where they can make a meaningful impact, such as education, healthcare, environmental sustainability, and economic development. This involves engaging with stakeholders to understand their needs and expectations, setting clear goals and metrics for measuring progress, and transparently reporting on CSR activities and outcomes. Ethical leadership ensures that CSR initiatives are genuine and impactful, avoiding superficial or token efforts that merely serve as public relations exercises.

Ethical leaders recognize that CSR is not a one-time effort but an ongoing commitment to continuous improvement. They cultivate a culture of social responsibility within their organizations, empowering employees to contribute to CSR initiatives and encouraging innovation in addressing social and environmental challenges. This includes providing training and resources, fostering collaboration across departments, and recognizing and rewarding ethical behavior. By embedding CSR into the fabric of their organizations, ethical leaders create a lasting legacy of positive impact and sustainability.

The benefits of CSR and ethical leadership extend beyond enhanced reputation and brand loyalty. Companies that prioritize ethical behavior and social responsibility are better positioned to attract and retain top talent, as employees increasingly seek purpose-driven work environments. Additionally, ethical companies are more resilient in the face of regulatory changes, market fluctuations, and reputational risks. By embracing CSR and ethical leadership, businesses can navigate the complexities of the modern world with integrity and purpose, ensuring long-term success and sustainability.

6

Chapter 6: The Role of Ethics in Marketing and Advertising

Marketing and advertising play a crucial role in shaping consumer perceptions and driving business growth. However, ethical considerations are paramount in ensuring that marketing practices are honest, transparent, and respectful of consumer rights. Ethical marketing involves presenting truthful information, avoiding deceptive claims, and respecting consumer privacy. It requires a commitment to fairness, inclusivity, and social responsibility, ensuring that marketing efforts contribute positively to society and do not exploit or manipulate consumers.

One of the key ethical challenges in marketing is balancing persuasive techniques with honesty and transparency. While marketing aims to influence consumer behavior, it must do so without resorting to deceptive practices or misleading claims. This includes providing accurate and complete information about products and services, clearly disclosing terms and conditions, and avoiding hidden fees or charges. Ethical marketers prioritize the trust and well-being of their customers, recognizing that long-term relationships are built on honesty and integrity.

Inclusivity and diversity are also essential components of ethical marketing. Marketing campaigns should reflect and respect the diverse backgrounds and experiences of consumers, avoiding stereotypes, biases, and discrimination.

This involves using inclusive language and imagery, considering the needs and preferences of diverse consumer groups, and promoting products and services that contribute to social and environmental well-being. By embracing inclusivity and diversity, ethical marketers can create campaigns that resonate with a broad audience and contribute to a more equitable and just society.

The ethical use of consumer data is another critical consideration in modern marketing. With the advent of digital technology, businesses have access to vast amounts of consumer data, enabling highly targeted and personalized marketing efforts. However, this requires a commitment to data privacy and security, ensuring that consumer data is collected, used, and shared responsibly. Ethical marketers obtain informed consent, provide clear and transparent privacy policies, and prioritize the protection of consumer data. By adopting ethical data practices, businesses can build trust and foster positive relationships with their customers.

7

Chapter 7: Ethical Decision-Making in the Digital Age

The digital age has transformed the way businesses operate, offering new opportunities for innovation, growth, and efficiency. However, it has also introduced complex ethical challenges that require careful consideration and responsible decision-making. Ethical decision-making in the digital age involves navigating issues such as data privacy, cybersecurity, artificial intelligence, and the digital divide. Businesses must adopt ethical frameworks and principles to guide their actions, ensuring that they leverage digital technologies for the greater good while mitigating potential risks and harms.

Data privacy is a paramount ethical concern in the digital age. Businesses collect and process vast amounts of personal data, raising questions about consent, transparency, and the responsible use of data. Ethical decision-making requires businesses to prioritize data privacy, obtain informed consent, and provide clear and transparent privacy policies. This includes implementing robust data security measures to protect against breaches and unauthorized access, as well as ensuring that data is used ethically and in line with consumer expectations.

Cybersecurity is another critical ethical consideration in the digital age. As businesses increasingly rely on digital technologies, they must protect their systems and data from cyber threats and attacks. Ethical decision-making involves adopting best practices for cybersecurity, such as regular security assessments, employee training, and incident response plans. Businesses must also collaborate with industry peers, regulators, and cybersecurity experts to stay informed about emerging threats and develop effective strategies for mitigating risks. By prioritizing cybersecurity, businesses can ensure the integrity and resilience of their digital operations.

Artificial intelligence (AI) and automation present both opportunities and ethical challenges for businesses. While AI can enhance efficiency, productivity, and decision-making, it also raises concerns about bias, transparency, and accountability. Ethical decision-making involves developing and implementing AI systems that are fair, transparent, and accountable, ensuring that they do not perpetuate or exacerbate existing inequalities. This includes conducting ethical impact assessments, engaging with diverse stakeholders, and adopting guidelines and standards for responsible AI development and use. By embracing ethical principles, businesses can leverage AI and automation to drive innovation and positive change while addressing potential risks and harms.

The digital divide is an important ethical issue that businesses must address in the digital age. Access to digital technologies and the internet is not evenly distributed, with significant disparities based on factors such as geography, socioeconomic status, and education. Ethical decision-making involves recognizing and addressing these disparities, ensuring that digital innovations are accessible and inclusive. This includes investing in digital literacy programs, supporting initiatives to expand internet access, and designing products and services that cater to diverse needs and preferences. By addressing the digital divide, businesses can contribute to a more equitable and inclusive digital economy.

8

Chapter 8: Building an Ethical Corporate Culture

An ethical corporate culture is the foundation of sustainable business success. It involves fostering a work environment where ethical behavior is valued, encouraged, and rewarded. Building an ethical corporate culture requires a commitment from leadership, clear ethical guidelines and policies, ongoing training and education, and mechanisms for accountability and transparency. By cultivating an ethical culture, businesses can create a positive and supportive work environment, enhance employee morale and engagement, and build trust with stakeholders.

Leadership plays a crucial role in shaping an ethical corporate culture. Ethical leaders set the tone for the organization, modeling ethical behavior and decision-making. They communicate the importance of ethics and integrity, establish clear ethical guidelines and policies, and hold themselves and others accountable for upholding ethical standards. By demonstrating a commitment to ethics, leaders inspire employees to act responsibly and make ethical decisions in their daily work.

Clear ethical guidelines and policies are essential for building an ethical corporate culture. These guidelines should outline the organization's values, principles, and expectations for ethical behavior. They should provide guidance on common ethical dilemmas and decision-making processes, as well as mechanisms for reporting and addressing ethical concerns. By establishing clear ethical guidelines, businesses can create a shared understanding of what constitutes ethical behavior and provide employees with the tools and resources they need to act ethically.

Ongoing training and education are critical for reinforcing an ethical corporate culture. Employees should receive regular training on ethical guidelines, policies, and best practices, as well as opportunities to discuss and reflect on ethical issues. This includes training on topics such as data privacy, cybersecurity, diversity and inclusion, and responsible innovation. By providing ongoing education, businesses can ensure that employees are informed and equipped to navigate ethical challenges and make responsible decisions.

Mechanisms for accountability and transparency are essential for maintaining an ethical corporate culture. This includes establishing processes for reporting and addressing ethical concerns, conducting regular ethical audits and assessments, and fostering open communication and dialogue. Businesses should create a safe and supportive environment where employees feel comfortable raising ethical issues and concerns without fear of retaliation. By promoting accountability and transparency, businesses can build trust and ensure that ethical behavior is consistently upheld across the organization.

9

Chapter 9: Ethical Supply Chain Management

Ethical supply chain management is essential for ensuring that business operations are sustainable, transparent, and socially responsible. It involves adopting practices that prioritize human rights, environmental sustainability, and ethical labor conditions throughout the supply chain. By fostering ethical supply chain management, businesses can build trust with stakeholders, enhance their reputation, and contribute to positive social and environmental outcomes.

One of the key components of ethical supply chain management is ensuring fair labor practices. This includes prohibiting child labor, forced labor, and discrimination, as well as providing fair wages, safe working conditions, and opportunities for employee development. Businesses must conduct regular audits and assessments of their suppliers to ensure compliance with ethical labor standards. By prioritizing fair labor practices, companies can support the well-being of workers and contribute to social justice.

Environmental sustainability is another critical aspect of ethical supply chain management. Businesses must adopt practices that minimize their environmental impact, such as reducing waste, conserving resources, and promoting the use of sustainable materials. This involves collaborating with suppliers to implement environmentally friendly practices, such as energy-efficient production methods, waste reduction initiatives, and sustainable sourcing. By prioritizing environmental sustainability, businesses can contribute to the protection of natural resources and the well-being of future generations.

Transparency and traceability are essential for ethical supply chain management. Businesses must provide clear and accurate information about their supply chain practices, including sourcing, production, and distribution processes. This involves implementing traceability systems that allow stakeholders to track the origin and journey of products, as well as providing regular updates on supply chain performance and progress. By fostering transparency and traceability, businesses can build trust with consumers and stakeholders, demonstrating their commitment to ethical practices.

Collaboration and partnerships are key to fostering ethical supply chain management. Businesses must work closely with suppliers, industry peers, and non-governmental organizations (NGOs) to develop and implement ethical standards and practices. This includes engaging in multi-stakeholder initiatives, sharing best practices, and supporting capacity-building efforts for suppliers. By fostering collaboration and partnerships, businesses can drive positive change and create a more ethical and sustainable supply chain.

10

Chapter 10: The Importance of Ethics in Corporate Governance

Corporate governance refers to the system by which companies are directed and controlled. Ethical corporate governance is essential for ensuring that businesses operate with integrity, transparency, and accountability. It involves establishing clear governance structures, defining roles and responsibilities, and implementing practices that promote ethical behavior and decision-making. By prioritizing ethical corporate governance, businesses can build trust with stakeholders, enhance their reputation, and ensure long-term success.

One of the key components of ethical corporate governance is establishing clear governance structures. This includes defining the roles and responsibilities of the board of directors, executive management, and other key stakeholders. Governance structures should promote accountability, transparency, and ethical decision-making, ensuring that the interests of all stakeholders are considered. By establishing clear governance structures, businesses can create a strong foundation for ethical behavior and effective decision-making.

Transparency and accountability are essential for ethical corporate governance. Businesses must provide clear and accurate information about their operations, performance, and decision-making processes. This includes regular financial reporting, disclosure of conflicts of interest, and transparent communication with stakeholders. By fostering transparency and accountability, businesses can build trust and credibility, demonstrating their commitment to ethical practices.

Ethical corporate governance also involves promoting a culture of integrity and responsibility. This includes establishing ethical guidelines and policies, providing ongoing training and education, and fostering open communication and dialogue. Businesses must create an environment where ethical behavior is valued and rewarded, and where employees feel empowered to raise ethical concerns without fear of retaliation. By promoting a culture of integrity, businesses can ensure that ethical behavior is consistently upheld across the organization.

Stakeholder engagement is a critical aspect of ethical corporate governance. Businesses must actively engage with stakeholders, including shareholders, employees, customers, suppliers, and communities, to understand their needs and expectations. This involves seeking feedback, addressing concerns, and involving stakeholders in decision-making processes. By fostering stakeholder engagement, businesses can build strong relationships and ensure that their governance practices align with the values and interests of their stakeholders.

11

Chapter 11: Ethical Considerations in Financial Management

Financial management is a critical aspect of business operations, involving the planning, organizing, and controlling of financial resources. Ethical considerations are paramount in ensuring that financial practices are transparent, fair, and responsible. Ethical financial management involves adhering to principles of honesty, integrity, and accountability, ensuring that financial decisions align with the values and goals of the organization. By prioritizing ethical financial management, businesses can build trust with stakeholders, enhance their reputation, and ensure long-term financial stability.

One of the key components of ethical financial management is transparency. Businesses must provide clear and accurate information about their financial performance, including financial statements, budgets, and forecasts. This involves adhering to accounting standards and practices, conducting regular audits and assessments, and providing transparent communication with stakeholders. By prioritizing transparency, businesses can build trust and credibility, demonstrating their commitment to ethical financial practices.

Integrity is another critical aspect of ethical financial management. This involves ensuring that financial decisions are honest, fair, and aligned with the values and goals of the organization. Ethical financial management requires businesses to avoid conflicts of interest, insider trading, and fraudulent activities. By prioritizing integrity, businesses can create a culture of ethical behavior and ensure that financial practices are responsible and accountable.

Accountability is essential for ethical financial management. Businesses must establish clear roles and responsibilities for financial decision-making, ensuring that individuals and teams are held accountable for their actions. This involves implementing checks and balances, conducting regular reviews and assessments, and providing mechanisms for reporting and addressing ethical concerns. By fostering accountability, businesses can ensure that financial practices are aligned with ethical principles and contribute to the overall well-being of the organization.

Ethical financial management also involves considering the broader social and environmental impact of financial decisions. This includes prioritizing sustainable investments, supporting ethical business practices, and promoting social responsibility. Businesses must adopt practices that contribute to positive social and environmental outcomes, such as responsible investing, ethical sourcing, and philanthropic efforts. By integrating ethical considerations into financial management, businesses can create value that extends beyond financial gains and contributes to the greater good.

12

Chapter 12: Balancing Profit and Purpose

Balancing profit and purpose is a key challenge for businesses in the modern world. While financial success is essential for sustaining operations and growth, businesses must also consider their broader impact on society and the environment. Ethical businesses prioritize both profit and purpose, ensuring that their operations contribute to positive social and environmental outcomes. By balancing profit and purpose, businesses can build trust with stakeholders, enhance their reputation, and ensure long-term success and sustainability.

One of the key components of balancing profit and purpose is adopting a stakeholder-inclusive approach. This involves considering the interests of all stakeholders, including shareholders, employees, customers, suppliers, and communities, in decision-making processes. Ethical businesses prioritize the well-being of their stakeholders, ensuring that their operations are fair, transparent, and responsible. By adopting a stakeholder-inclusive approach, businesses can create value that benefits all stakeholders and contributes to the overall well-being of society.

Sustainability is another critical aspect of balancing profit and purpose. Ethical businesses adopt practices that minimize their environmental impact and promote the well-being of future generations. This includes reducing waste, conserving resources, and promoting the use of sustainable materials. By prioritizing sustainability, businesses can create long-term value that extends beyond financial gains and contributes to the protection of natural resources and the well-being of future generations.

Social responsibility is essential for balancing profit and purpose. Ethical businesses prioritize the well-being of communities, supporting initiatives that address social and economic challenges. This includes investing in education, healthcare, and economic development, as well as supporting ethical labor practices and fair wages. By prioritizing social responsibility, businesses can create positive social outcomes and contribute to the overall well-being of society.

Collaboration and partnerships are key to balancing profit and purpose. Businesses must work closely with stakeholders, including industry peers, non-governmental organizations (NGOs), and government agencies, to develop and implement ethical practices. This includes engaging in multi-stakeholder initiatives, sharing best practices, and supporting capacity-building efforts for suppliers and communities. By fostering collaboration and partnerships, businesses can drive positive change and create a more ethical and sustainable world.

13

Chapter 13: Ethics in Technology and Innovation

The rapid advancement of technology and innovation brings both opportunities and ethical challenges. Businesses must navigate the ethical implications of emerging technologies, such as artificial intelligence, blockchain, biotechnology, and the Internet of Things (IoT). Ethical considerations in technology and innovation involve ensuring that technological advancements are developed and deployed responsibly, transparently, and with respect for human rights and societal values. By prioritizing ethics in technology and innovation, businesses can foster trust, promote positive societal impact, and mitigate potential risks and harms.

Artificial intelligence (AI) is one of the most transformative technologies of our time, offering significant benefits in various industries, from healthcare to finance to transportation. However, AI also raises ethical concerns, such as bias, privacy, and accountability. Ethical considerations in AI involve ensuring that AI systems are designed and trained to be fair, transparent, and accountable. This includes addressing biases in data and algorithms, protecting individual privacy, and ensuring that AI decisions can be explained and justified. By adopting ethical principles in AI development and deployment, businesses can harness the potential of AI while minimizing its risks.

Blockchain technology offers transparency, security, and decentralization, making it a valuable tool for various applications, such as supply chain management, finance, and healthcare. However, ethical considerations in blockchain involve ensuring that its use aligns with societal values and regulatory standards. This includes addressing issues related to data privacy, security, and the environmental impact of blockchain networks. Ethical blockchain practices involve implementing safeguards to protect data, ensuring compliance with regulations, and adopting sustainable energy solutions. By prioritizing ethics in blockchain, businesses can leverage its benefits while addressing its challenges.

Biotechnology, including genetic engineering, personalized medicine, and synthetic biology, holds great promise for improving human health and well-being. However, it also raises ethical questions related to safety, consent, and the potential for unintended consequences. Ethical considerations in biotechnology involve ensuring that research and development are conducted responsibly, with respect for individual rights and societal values. This includes obtaining informed consent, conducting thorough risk assessments, and ensuring transparency in research processes. By adopting ethical principles in biotechnology, businesses can contribute to advancements in healthcare while addressing ethical concerns.

The Internet of Things (IoT) connects devices and systems, enabling greater efficiency, automation, and data collection. However, IoT raises ethical concerns related to data privacy, security, and the potential for surveillance. Ethical considerations in IoT involve ensuring that devices and systems are designed and deployed with privacy and security in mind. This includes implementing robust data protection measures, obtaining informed consent, and ensuring transparency in data collection and use. By prioritizing ethics in IoT, businesses can create a connected world that respects individual rights and promotes societal well-being.

14

Chapter 14: Navigating Ethical Challenges in the Global Economy

The global economy presents both opportunities and ethical challenges for businesses. Navigating these challenges requires a commitment to ethical principles, cultural awareness, and responsible decision-making. Ethical considerations in the global economy involve addressing issues such as labor rights, environmental sustainability, fair trade, and social justice. By adopting ethical practices and collaborating with stakeholders, businesses can navigate the complexities of the global economy with integrity and purpose.

Labor rights are a critical ethical concern in the global economy. Businesses must ensure that their operations and supply chains respect the rights and well-being of workers. This includes prohibiting child labor, forced labor, and discrimination, as well as providing fair wages, safe working conditions, and opportunities for employee development. Ethical labor practices involve conducting regular audits and assessments, engaging with workers and labor organizations, and implementing policies that promote fairness and justice. By prioritizing labor rights, businesses can contribute to social justice and the well-being of workers.

Environmental sustainability is another critical ethical consideration in the global economy. Businesses must adopt practices that minimize their environmental impact and promote the well-being of future generations. This includes reducing waste, conserving resources, and promoting the use of sustainable materials. Ethical environmental practices involve collaborating with stakeholders, implementing sustainable sourcing and production methods, and supporting initiatives that protect natural resources. By prioritizing environmental sustainability, businesses can contribute to the protection of the planet and the well-being of future generations.

Fair trade is essential for ensuring that global trade practices are ethical and responsible. This involves promoting trade policies and practices that are fair, transparent, and equitable. Ethical fair trade practices include ensuring that producers and suppliers receive fair compensation, supporting sustainable and ethical sourcing, and promoting economic development in marginalized communities. By adopting fair trade principles, businesses can create positive social and economic outcomes and contribute to a more just and equitable global economy.

Social justice is a key ethical consideration in the global economy. Businesses must address issues related to inequality, discrimination, and access to resources and opportunities. This includes promoting diversity and inclusion, supporting initiatives that address social and economic disparities, and advocating for policies that promote social justice. Ethical social justice practices involve engaging with stakeholders, supporting community development, and implementing policies that promote fairness and equality. By prioritizing social justice, businesses can contribute to a more inclusive and equitable global economy.

15

Chapter 15: The Role of Ethics in Crisis Management

Crisis management is a critical aspect of business operations, involving the identification, assessment, and response to potential threats and disruptions. Ethical considerations are paramount in ensuring that crisis management practices are responsible, transparent, and aligned with the values of the organization. Ethical crisis management involves prioritizing the well-being of stakeholders, ensuring transparent communication, and making decisions that are fair and just. By adopting ethical principles in crisis management, businesses can build trust, enhance their reputation, and ensure resilience in the face of challenges.

One of the key components of ethical crisis management is prioritizing the well-being of stakeholders. This involves identifying and addressing the needs and concerns of employees, customers, suppliers, and communities. Ethical crisis management requires businesses to act with compassion, empathy, and responsibility, ensuring that their actions prioritize the well-being of those affected by the crisis. This includes providing support and resources, addressing concerns and grievances, and ensuring that decisions are made with the best interests of stakeholders in mind.

Transparency and communication are essential for ethical crisis management. Businesses must provide clear, accurate, and timely information about the crisis, including its causes, impacts, and response efforts. This involves maintaining open lines of communication with stakeholders, addressing misinformation and rumors, and providing regular updates on the status of the crisis and response efforts. By prioritizing transparency and communication, businesses can build trust and credibility, demonstrating their commitment to ethical crisis management.

Ethical decision-making is critical in crisis management. This involves making decisions that are fair, just, and aligned with the values of the organization. Ethical crisis management requires businesses to consider the long-term implications of their decisions, including potential impacts on stakeholders, the environment, and society. This includes conducting ethical impact assessments, engaging with diverse stakeholders, and adopting a principled approach to decision-making. By prioritizing ethical decision-making, businesses can ensure that their crisis management practices are responsible and aligned with their values.

Collaboration and partnership are key to effective and ethical crisis management. Businesses must work closely with stakeholders, including government agencies, non-governmental organizations (NGOs), industry peers, and communities, to develop and implement effective crisis response strategies. This includes sharing information, resources, and best practices, as well as coordinating efforts to address the crisis and mitigate its impacts. By fostering collaboration and partnership, businesses can enhance their resilience and ensure that their crisis management practices are ethical and effective.

16

Chapter 16: The Future of Business Ethics

The future of business ethics is shaped by emerging trends, technologies, and societal values. As the business landscape continues to evolve, ethical considerations will play an increasingly important role in shaping corporate strategies, decision-making processes, and stakeholder relationships. Businesses must stay informed about emerging ethical challenges and opportunities, adopt proactive and responsible practices, and demonstrate a commitment to ethical principles. By embracing the future of business ethics, businesses can navigate the complexities of the modern world with integrity and purpose.

One of the key trends shaping the future of business ethics is the rise of stakeholder capitalism. This involves prioritizing the interests of all stakeholders, including shareholders, employees, customers, suppliers, and communities, in decision-making processes. Stakeholder capitalism recognizes that businesses have a responsibility to contribute to the well-being of society and the environment, beyond generating profits. By adopting a stakeholder-inclusive approach, businesses can create value that benefits all stakeholders and contributes to positive social and environmental outcomes.

The integration of technology and ethics will play a critical role in the future of business ethics. Emerging technologies, such as artificial intelligence, blockchain, biotechnology, and the Internet of Things (IoT), offer significant opportunities for innovation and growth. However, they also raise ethical concerns related to privacy, security, bias, and accountability. Businesses must adopt ethical frameworks and principles to guide the development and deployment of new technologies, ensuring that they align with societal values and promote positive outcomes. By prioritizing ethics in technology, businesses can harness the potential of innovation while addressing its challenges.

Sustainability and social responsibility will continue to be central to the future of business ethics. Businesses must adopt practices that minimize their environmental impact, promote the well-being of future generations, and address social and economic disparities. This includes investing in sustainable technologies and practices, supporting initiatives that promote social justice and economic development, and advocating for policies that protect the environment and promote fairness and equality. By prioritizing sustainability and social responsibility, businesses can contribute to a more just and sustainable world.

Ethical leadership will be essential for navigating the future of business ethics. Ethical leaders set the tone for their organizations, modeling ethical behavior and decision-making, and fostering a culture of integrity and responsibility. They prioritize transparency, accountability, and stakeholder engagement, ensuring that their actions align with ethical principles. By demonstrating a commitment to ethics, ethical leaders inspire employees, build trust with stakeholders, and guide their organizations toward long-term success and sustainability.

17

Chapter 17: Embracing Ethical Principles for a Better Future

Embracing ethical principles is essential for creating a better future for businesses, society, and the environment. Ethical principles, such as integrity, transparency, accountability, and social responsibility, guide businesses in making decisions that align with their values and contribute to positive outcomes. By prioritizing ethical principles, businesses can build trust with stakeholders, enhance their reputation, and ensure long-term success and sustainability.

Integrity is the foundation of ethical behavior. Businesses that prioritize integrity act with honesty, fairness, and respect for others. This involves making decisions that are aligned with ethical values, avoiding conflicts of interest, and maintaining transparency in all aspects of operations. By prioritizing integrity, businesses can build trust with stakeholders and create a culture of ethical behavior.

Transparency is essential for building trust and credibility. Businesses that prioritize transparency provide clear and accurate information about their operations, performance, and decision-making processes. This includes regular financial reporting, disclosure of conflicts of interest, and open communication with stakeholders. By fostering transparency, businesses can demonstrate their commitment to ethical practices and build strong relationships with stakeholders.

Accountability is critical for ensuring that ethical principles are consistently upheld. Businesses that prioritize accountability establish clear roles and responsibilities, conduct regular audits and assessments, and provide mechanisms for reporting and addressing ethical concerns. This involves holding individuals and teams accountable for their actions and ensuring that decisions are made in line with ethical values. By fostering accountability, businesses can ensure that their operations are responsible and aligned with ethical principles.

Social responsibility is essential for contributing to the well-being of society and the environment. Businesses that prioritize social responsibility adopt practices that minimize their environmental impact, promote the well-being of future generations, and address social and economic disparities. This includes investing in sustainable technologies and practices, supporting initiatives that promote social justice and economic development, and advocating for policies that protect the environment and promote fairness and equality. By prioritizing social responsibility, businesses can create positive social and environmental outcomes and contribute to a better future.

Book Description:

In "The Ethical Edge: Balancing Innovation, Psychology, and Cultural Awareness in Business," readers are invited to explore the critical role of ethics in the modern business landscape. This insightful book delves into the complexities of ethical considerations across various aspects of business, including innovation, consumer psychology, cultural awareness, corporate social responsibility, marketing, financial management, and technology.

Through 17 thoughtfully crafted chapters, the book provides a comprehensive examination of ethical principles and practices that guide businesses in making responsible and impactful decisions. From understanding the evolution of business ethics to navigating ethical challenges in the global economy, readers will gain valuable insights into how businesses can balance profit and purpose while contributing to positive social and environmental outcomes.

"The Ethical Edge" emphasizes the importance of ethical leadership,

CHAPTER 17: EMBRACING ETHICAL PRINCIPLES FOR A BETTER FUTURE

transparency, accountability, and social responsibility, offering practical strategies for fostering an ethical corporate culture and ensuring resilience in the face of challenges. With a focus on embracing ethical principles for a better future, this book serves as a valuable resource for business leaders, professionals, and anyone interested in the intersection of ethics and business.

www.ingramcontent.com/pod-product-compliance
Lightning Source LLC
LaVergne TN
LVHW010441070526
838199LV00066B/6131